AN ADDRESS

DELIVERED BEFORE THE

GRADUATING CLASS

OF THE

LAW DEPARTMENT

OF THE

UNIVERSITY OF MICHIGAN,

March 28, 1866.

By JAMES V. CAMPBELL,

ONE OF THE JUSTICES OF THE SUPREME COURT OF MICHIGAN, AND MARSHALL PROFESSOR
OF LAW.

PUBLISHED AT THE REQUEST OF THE CLASS.

DETROIT:
F. A. SCHOBER & BRO., PRINTERS, LARNED STREET.
1866.

Law and Lawyers in Society.

We have spent some pleasant time together in searching out the foundations of the law. In studying its principles, you have also acquired, I trust, a creditable amount of knowledge upon the special topics which are most likely to claim the attention of active lawyers. And the time has now come, in which, as we are about separating, we may all of us pause a moment, to consider to what end we have been following our common labors, and what use is to come of your discipline and acquirements. The years of early manhood are not given to be wasted, and the energies of earnest and hopeful natures are too precious to be thrown away. If our occupation here has had no certain and worthy aim, it can give us no pleasure to review it.

We have all been persuaded that it was worth while to devote ourselves to our work, and that our ends were not without worthiness. Let us again consider them at this definite stage of our progress, and judge them by the only test that is safe, their practical utility in the business of life. This business I understand to be, so living as to do our part in maintaining the best interests of society, as well as those of our immediate personal sphere, and in striving that no fault of ours shall cause any good course to be obstructed. Let us weigh, then, the value of the pursuit of jurisprudence, and endeavor to judge how far it tends to benefit men. In doing this, I propose, in my brief space, to do little more than indicate some of its higher capabilities in secular affairs.

There are two views in which every scientific pursuit presents itself to its votaries. Neither is low or altogether blame-worthy, and yet, when compared, their merits are very far apart. The one presents special knowledge as no more than an end in itself, the worthiness of which dignifies the toil by which it is reached, while its pleasantness makes every labor grateful. But, while personal pleasure and profit may very well be enjoyed, and may be necessary inducements to diligence, yet no amount of learning is of any great worth, if it cannot be made a means to further a valuable purpose. We are thrown together in society, as workmen in a common enterprise; and while, by the division of labor, each chooses, or has chosen for him, such work as he is best fitted for, his production is only supplemental to that of others. Each of us needs what is wrought by the rest, to make his own work available. If each worked alone, there could be no progress, and no improvement. But combined results are leading to unceasing advancement. The farmer feeds the miner, and the miner supplies the forge, and the forge produces the metal ready to be wrought. The man of science conceives the machine which his hands are not cunning to execute, and the mechanic, with his ready fingers and quick apprehension, grasps and executes the plan which he was not capable of devising; and the result of these joint labors and thoughts is some marvel of mechanism, which makes life easier for all of them, and advances society in physical and moral prosperity. The same analogy holds in labors not corporeal. Learning of one kind aids learning of a different kind; as the physician acquires medical knowledge, and the lawyer legal knowledge, and each man the lore of his calling, that the information society needs may be full and reliable. Some one in every department has given his labors to the perfection of his own favorite science, and they jointly cover the field. The importance of any pursuit, then, is measured very much by the extent to which it may be made available in the education or improvement of society. And it cannot be denied that, among all secular pursuits, the law meets more varied interests, and concerns more complications of human affairs than any other. Law is the only universal bond which protects and strengthens the minor bands of union among men. Property is its creature, all human associations need its sanctions, life and liberty have no security without it, and even an honest name may be exposed to remediless peril without its protection.

But the magnitude of its theatre and the extent of its combinations admonish us, that the study of a subject which pervades all human institutions is no scholastic exercise, to be completed by the labor of a few of the opening years of life. Our utmost aim, in a course of legal instruction, cannot reach beyond preparation. If you have been enabled to learn how to apply yourselves to the solution of such questions as may arise in the future, and how to search readily the repositories of the law; in short, if you can now devote yourselves with some degree of facility to the study which must henceforth occupy your laborious lives, you have made a good use of your time. If you should imagine that you have mastered enough of the law to dispense with further study, you would show a strange misconception of your chosen profession, which would prove your unfitness for any of its walks. Even in those subterranean regions of legal practice, through which miserable reptiles crawl amid filth and vermin, there are labyrinths to be explored, and dim passages, not mapped on any chart, discovered day by day by those unhappy dwellers in darkness.

Neither will you act wisely, if you think you may safely choose a few legal topics, and devote your entire thoughts to them. The law concerns all the interests of human life and conduct; and its principles are so interlaced in one fabric, that each depends on, and is supported by, the rest. A complete knowledge of one department requires a complete knowledge of all; and in that moderate advance which most persons must be content with making, the same result appears in its degree. Unless we realize at the outset the connection and inter-dependence of the various parts of the law, we can never make any satisfactory progress. Nor can we succeed without recognizing the further fact, that all science and learning are its associates and helps. All liberal culture is a positive and direct aid to legal knowledge; and some degree of acquirement has always been considered a necessity.

Sir Henry Finch, who asserts to himself the honor of having first reduced into an orderly system the scattered rules of the Common Law of England, does not hesitate, in tracing it back to its origin, to include within its foundation principles all the elements of human learning, as well as the laws of conscience and the deductions of sound reason. "The sparks of all sciences in the world," said he, "are enveloped in the ashes of the law: so that it was well said by one,—' not from the edicts of the Prætor, nor from the twelve tables, but from the inmost depths of philosophy, must be drawn the discipline of the law.' He who would bring before him the whole body of the law, and go deeply and prudently therein, must not lay the foundation of his edifice on estates, tenures, and writs, but on the living and healthy principles with which our books are filled." * Such was the teaching of those great masters, whose solid learning and plain sense built up the only system which has ever resulted in free government; and if some of their successors for a time allowed themselves to lose sight of the dignity of their calling, the reproach has been long since wiped away. The modern English bar would be an ornament to any age; and the countrymen of Marshall, and Kent, and Story, will acknowledge the value of those broad views which built up our Republic on a sure and firm basis, and made the forum a striving place for the champions of earnest principle, instead of a stage for limber mountebanks.

As each man's course in life is laudable in proportion to its general usefulness, and as governments are the most important of all human institutions, the aim of the lawyer should always be to make himself a good citizen. The safety and prosperity of all governments must depend on private virtue and intelligence; but in no country is this so obvious as in a Republic. And the plan of our Commonwealth has made its security depend very much upon the learning and integrity of those who have devoted themselves to the study of the Law. In other countries there are powers and

---

* Description del Common Leys Dangleterre, fol. 3.

systems only regulated by the will of the government. The unwritten constitution of England is subject, in fact, to the unqualified control of Parliament, which is not, like our Assemblies, a legislative body only, but represents in itself the supreme and complete authority of the realm; and the whole system has been modified at its pleasure. Yet, even in that country, radical changes are rarely made, and questions of private and public law have become settled by the wisdom of legal authorities.

Our country affords the first instance in which the various departments of government have been organized and regulated by a law binding them all, in which the people, not content with holding their agents to a strict account, have bound themselves also, and guarded their institutions from the dangers of their own passions and caprices. Our Supreme Law is a written law. It cannot be transgressed by the people, any more than by their government. They may change it, but only after time has been given for separate and calm reflection.

Whenever, therefore, any department of government is called upon to act, it finds the path marked out for it, either by grants, or by limitations, which are never shifting, and never unknown. If varying judgments arrive at different constructions, the original rule is always at hand to test them, and no comments can vary it. And every citizen, who is called upon to exercise any franchise, from that of voting to that of governing, is bound to qualify himself for his functions, by obtaining an understanding of the true character of his government. Its framework is simple enough to be understood by all men of common intelligence, but no institution framed by man, — still less one made perfect by the teachings of History, — can be known by intuition. It is based on sense and virtue; and where those are wanting it can never be fairly comprehended. No question can arise, concerning the correctness of any form of public action, which does not, in this country, present combined issues of law and statesmanship. Our constitutions separate the three great departments of government, which were never absolutely separated before. To disentangle from the precedents of the past the executive or judicial functions, and separate them from the legislative, or to distinguish either from the reserved powers which lie behind them all, is a task calling for the highest wisdom and the profoundest learning. Yet, whenever the humblest citizen, while the peaceful course of affairs continues, suffers personal loss or injury from what he conceives to be an excess of authority in any of these departments, he can compel the judiciary to enter upon this task, and to say upon their consciences whether or no there has been any deviation from its constitutional path. And this liability, to respond to such momentous inquiries, renders it necessary that these questions should be among those daily pondered, and continually investigated. It requires something more than a comparison of precedents; because precise precedents are not to be found, for cases arising out of a new order of affairs. Nothing can be useful here but a search into the profound principles on which government is based. If capable of being anticipated and uniformly regulated in advance, such regulation may naturally belong to one department. If action must be modified or governed by events, incapable of regulation, and urgent for decisive measures, it as naturally falls into another. To aid these inquiries, the customary experience of great nations must be made available; the mind must grasp, and turn from side to side, the whole plan of affairs, and study the whole range of possibilities and chances, and must appreciate all presumable consequences. The prosperity of every organized community requires a sound construction of its organic law; and no one can over-rate the danger of leaving its settlement to the conceit of ignorance, or the madness of prejudice and the blindness of obstinacy. No living member of the public body can be paralysed or dwarfed in its powers, without general suffering. The political, like the natural body, requires the full enjoyment of all its functions, and suffers with every suffering portion. When any one assumes oracular credit on such vital questions as these,—(and all men are called upon to consider them)—he needs all the vigor of his intellect—all the knowledge which diligence can acquire—all the prudence which vigilance can teach him— all the honesty which an enlightened conscience can bestow— all the devotion of unselfish patriotism—and all that sympathy with the great common heart of the people, which can make him feel and express their settled and sober conclusions, which seldom fail of being profoundly just and true.

It has been observed, with more or less surprise, that the popular sentiment has sooner or later become fixed concerning all of the important problems of government which have arisen. This should be no matter of astonishment, when we consider that all free institutions are but the expression of the general will. Yet it is always hard to comprehend how a community, the mass of whose citizens, singly, would not be capable of rigidly trying and canvassing any vexed question of statesmanship, does generally arrive at the truth. The reason is, no doubt, because, with most of the community, the final decision arrived at has been by means of weighing and reviewing the suggestions and arguments of the few persons who can throw light upon the subject. All matters of human policy must be within the capacity of such intelligent minds as have not already been warped, by habit or prejudice, so as to be unfitted to receive them. But until some one gives an idea shape and expression, it cannot circulate among men. Ideas on these subjects can only come from those who have pondered them, and safe ideas can only be expected from those who have extensive knowledge, or much familiarity with the matters involved. When such persons define and set forth their conceptions, they have, in each mind, a tribunal ready to judge them. If they have the rare faculty of so presenting their thoughts, as by their statement alone to embody also their reasons and supports, the honest mind receiving the statements can determine at once their truth or fallacy. If true, they strike home as forcibly as if they were intuitions; and thereafter no doubt or uneasiness can arise concerning them. But this transparency does not characterize the expressions of most persons. In a majority of instances the clear expression is arrived at only as a final

result of amendment and criticism, and the subject is passed
from one to another, and many imperfect utterances are made
and forgotten, before the truth becomes manifest. This discussion is, in the main, confined to a few disputants. Most
of the community listen and weigh until they are satisfied.
They must receive assertions where they have no means of
trying them, except by their faith in the men who make them.
This faith will not be yielded to all; nor will any one be
trusted long, who has been detected in making unfounded
statements. They look for light to those most familiar with
the thing in hand; and it is to lawyers that attention is always turned, when subjects are opened which are dependent
on the interpretation of the law. Whether the tribunal of
judgment is the Bench or the people, there is little hope
of a safe conclusion, until the logic of the Bar has tried
every theory by the dry light of legal principles. But
so long as great questions remain unsettled, there is
danger of excess from passing excitements; and ideas are
snatched at as palatable, which, unless speedily exposed, will
accomplish mischief before any remedy can be applied to
counteract them. It is the duty of the Bar to stand in the
gap, and restrain contending passions by cool and sober
reason; and to inform themselves, and aid the community,
concerning all things of public moment which they find means
of studying and comprehending.

In approaching questions of public law, the lawyer must
always remember that they do not belong to the arbitrary
and technical portions of legal science, but are governed
by broad fundamental rules, which can only be applied
with a knowledge of human nature, and some correct no-
tions of statesmanship. The history of liberty has fur-
nished, indeed, many valuable precedents for determining
private rights; but questions immediately bearing upon
public interests present themselves under such varied
aspects, that we can seldom fall back, with entire confidence, upon any old adjudication to settle them. The
mere case-lawyer never appears to advantage in dealing
with such topics. They tax the best energies of those who

think for themselves, and who apply precedents only where their principles make them pertinent.

If there were no other office to be performed by the lawyer than that of being a good citizen, the nature of his pursuits would enable him, if true to himself, to render such good service to the public as few others can perform. And the unquestionable fact that, in spite of the ancient jests which have been traditionally aimed at him,—(but which have never broken his bones,)—he is always looked to for information upon vexed questions of public as well as private law, would be enough to vindicate the profession as one of the necessary pillars of the State. But the nature of his public services, and the character of the needful preparation for them, give to the science of jurisprudence a further and increased value, by enabling it to vindicate some pursuits, upon which the mass of men have often looked with coldness, and sometimes even with disapproval. It demonstrates the practical value of those studies which have no visible results, except in the improvement of the mind. Many things are studied with profit, where, to all appearance, they add little or nothing to the treasures of the memory for future expenditure in daily business. Because most persons live respectably and labor usefully without them, it is assumed that they are useless accomplishments, if not positively injurious dissipations. The instances are, happily, becoming rare, of respectable lawyers, who decry all other reading except their party papers, and the text-books from which they drew their inspiration in the days of dyspeptic digests. When human ingenuity or perverseness refuses to be bound in its lawlessness to go astray according to the recorded patterns of misbehavior, the occupation of those very scrupulous oracles is gone. If we never look upon their like again, let us receive the loss with becoming resignation.

It is no shame to any man that he has been compelled to enter life with slender preparation. He has the future before him. It is no credit to him if he refuses to make the most of that. The fruit of the grafted tree is as sweet as that of the seedling, from which the bud was taken ; but the flavor of the crab is not improved by time, and it will not grow unaided into a snow-apple. The list of great lawyers and statesmen contains the names of many who entered manhood with none but the rudiments of learning, but of not one who confined himself to the society of merely technical books. But how bright is the record of those benefactors of mankind, whose experience was varied, whose studies were as liberal as their opportunities permitted, and who subordinated all their pursuits to their advancement in sound and useful progress.

The great Roman lawyers were at once the best scholars and ablest publicists of their age; and when the Latin literature had been declining for some centuries from its Augustan purity, the great jurists still retained much of its pristine elegance and accuracy, and were far in advance of the other authors of their time. The personal faults of Bacon cannot deprive the world of the fruits of his manifold wisdom. Sir Matthew Hale has never ceased to be proverbial for his broad views and extensive learning, as well as his devoted piety; and no one can dispute his legal eminence. The liberal culture of Mansfield was the undoubted source of that preference of Common Law principle over senseless servility, which made him almost the founder of the modern law-merchant. Sir William Jones, when he wrote the most elegant treatise which has ever appeared on any ordinary branch of the law, found no hindrance in his great attainments. Blackstone, indeed, when he entered upon his legal career, took a solemn farewell of his muse, in a copy of atrocious verses; but she was evidently not one of the genuine maidens of Parnassus, and his immortal commentaries show plainly enough that he had not been deserted by all the nine. In our own day learning has most signally vindicated itself; and there are few prominent public men in Great Britain, who are not as well known for their scholarly accomplishments, as for their professional and business acquirements.

The Bar of America has also uniformly vindicated the value of a wide extent of knowledge and general culture. Without referring to the intellectual giants who have but lately passed away, it is by no means likely that Hamilton and Marshall will ever lose their hold on the admiration of our people. Unlike in temperament, they resembled each other in many of their prominent characteristics. Both were ardent and unselfish patriots, who gave up their youth to dangerous service, and achieved an honorable military renown. Both were friends and advisers of the Father of his Country, who drew much of his knowledge of public law from their clear and honest intellects. Both were statesmen in the broadest sense, and as ready in shaping as they were quick in conceiving policy. Both were profound thinkers, and learned in all the reasons as well as rules of the law, and whenever either of them traversed a field, there was nothing left behind for the gleaners. They brought home the weightiest principles of jurisprudence to the comprehension of the simplest understanding, and taught our people that knowledge of their institutions, which has kept the public heart sound, and the public head clear, against both well meaning and dishonest errors. Hamilton, though he died in his prime, had done, perhaps, his complete work. The great Chief Justice lived long enough to elucidate nearly all the vexed questions on which speculating visionaries had conjured up doubts, and then went calmly to his rest. No wiser man, no purer magistrate, no more modest or courteous gentleman, no better patriot, no truer believer, has adorned the seat of judgment. When we look at our triumphant country to-day, and remember how much of her safety is due to Marshall, we need no other evidence of the value of those pursuits, which enabled him to fulfil his mission.

But the pursuit of legal study has intrinsic merits. It cannot fail to enlarge the views, and elevate the character, of those who follow it with proper motives. The practice of the law has, indeed, its temptations, and many of its practitioners have undeniable faults. But the general character of the Bar, for integrity and public spirit, is not inferior to that of any profession or calling. Personal dissensions are not common among them, and envy and jealousy do not usually mar their intercourse. The tendency of the teachings of the law is certainly not calculated to induce any mean or treacherous conduct. Fidelity to his trusts is the constant lesson impressed upon the lawyer. He is always acting under the obligations of a public or private confidence. The sense of this obligation is habitual, and its violation is rare, and meets the sharpest censure.

There seems to be an idea prevalent in some quarters, that the lawyer is so continually brought in contact with the darker side of human nature, that the association is injurious to his own character, and prejudicial to his estimate of men. This is a great mistake. The majority of business does not usually consist in the defence of guilty criminals, and even there the aspect of crime is never attractive. But most litigation is between parties who cannot be said to be at all worse than the mass of mankind; and, for one case where there is actual dishonesty, there are many involving no moral turpitude. Moreover, even when men are guilty of wrong, it is no part of a lawyer's duty to justify that which is unjustifiable. But the amount of litigation prevented very much exceeds that which is commenced, and there is far more business done by most men in advising and arranging unlitigated affairs, than in lawsuits. And they deal with the good as well as the bad, and receive from men of all sorts such confidences as are entrusted to no other human ear. The lawyer sees what others cannot see, and can have very little about him of the necessary faculties of his office, if any phase of human nature is strange to him. And, for the honor of humanity, it must be said that he often sees things which if open to other eyes would surround many a desolate head with a saintly halo. If some men who walk in pride, and are respected by society, are known by him to be no better than whited sepulchres, he knows as well of generous self-denial, of long-suffering forbearance, of chivalrous devotion, of princely munificence. He sometimes sees youth hardened by the cold vices of maturer life, but he finds still oftener that age is not divested of the gentleness of youth, and is not unfaithful to the memories of childhood and early life. If some speculate upon the tragedies that are now and then unfolded before a counsellor, they may safely assume, also, that quieter and sweeter dramas are not strange to him. Those lawyers who have had the largest experience are not usually the most cynical. And those who have forced themselves into prominence by their talents, and yet been false men, have rarely left any permanent mark of their presence on the law. Aaron Burr was surpassed by few in acquirements or craft. He was Hamilton's professional rival, before he became his murderer. The records of the Courts, and the reported decisions, show that he was foremost among great men in the extent of his practice. But, except the historical fact of his prominence, he has left there no substantial memorial of his existence. He added nothing to jurisprudence. He took nothing from it. Justice was too pure to be defiled by him, and he was too vile to add anything to its treasures. The name of the wicked lawyer will rot as soon as that of any other villain, and he usually has the assurance, during life, that his brethren see through him, and thoroughly appreciate the disgrace of his company.

Instead of being injurious, his intercourse with men is one of the most valuable parts of a lawyer's experience. The study of mankind has always been justly regarded as the noblest of human pursuits. The whole course of human affairs, so far as they are susceptible of regulation at all, must be arranged with a due regard to human nature, or every plan is abortive. Laws which do not meet the general wants, or which violate the common feelings of the community, can never be enforced without disturbance. The words of wisdom addressed to one audience would be words of folly before another. In framing governments, even despots study out what their people will bear; and lovers of freedom inquire what the people will approve. All assume that these things can be ascertained, and that there are developments of motives, and passions, and prejudices, which must be thoroughly understood, before any system can be framed which will not offend them. We all know that this knowledge of men can only come from intimate contact, and that a knowledge of the general characteristics of communities can only be got at by intimately studying the peculiarities of all kinds and classes of people. This intimate acquaintance is never obtained by social intercourse alone. Most men of any considerable experience must know many individuals, whose reputation in society and among business men is very different. There are qualities that lie dormant until aroused by occasion. Society does not usually develope the meaner side of the avaricious and cruel; for self-esteem and hypocrisy are strong enough to counterbalance the moderate excitement such faults are likely to meet in general company. The usurer may be bland, and the tyrant sentimental, and the rogue may put on the guise of bluff and unceremonious honesty; and those who see through them all do not feel called upon to spoil social enjoyment, by exposing those whose exposure may grieve the innocent. And so one half of the community worship what the other half in equal honesty despise. The lawyer's occasions lead him to observe both the inner and outer life. He sees all kinds of people, under all manner of circumstances. He sees domestic tragedies and domestic comedies — the effects of prosperity and of adversity — the home countenance and the mask of society — the open and the closed chambers in men's bosoms; and, seeing them all, it is his own fault if he be not wiser for the seeing. The same occasions require him to become somewhat familiar with the idiosyncrasies of men in communities, or smaller companies. We all recognize the fact that nations have characters, as well as individuals. We do not always recognize what is equally true, but not so obvious, that this same principle prevails to some extent in all societies. And hence it is, that, while men may theorize as they will concerning political philosophy, and the abstract rules which would govern people very happily if they would only consent to be made happy in that way, no instance can be found in which the wisest closet philosopher has succeeded in framing a constitution or code, which would fit the people it was made for. Yet our own country can furnish instances enough of systems working very smoothly, which have been demonstrated by the same sort of philosophers to be extremely absurd. When we look at the complete crushing out of individuality, by the symmetrical codes which it has been in the power of some sovereigns to adopt, we have much reason to feel satisfied with our own systems, which may almost be said to have framed themselves. We see every day attempts made by sanguine reformers to make laws theoretically perfect. Divine laws are enforced in their perfection, by omniscience and omnipotence. Human laws can never be enforced on perfect principles, until men outgrow, in their perfection, the necessity of any human laws at all. The best proof of the value of human laws is in their results. Our own country and our mother country have grown free and powerful under an unwritten system, which was made up chiefly of nothing but popular usages, which became laws after, and not before, the people became accustomed to follow them. Our whole constitutional system is a mere development from recognized necessity. No one can understand human nature so well as to know what *will suit it*, as easily as to recognize what *has suited it*. But where there is an apparent demand for action, that wisdom which scorns to take into account the sentiments, and even the follies and caprices, as well as the interests of a community, is not a very exalted wisdom.

It is no reproach then, but rather an honor, to the law, that it compels its ministers to become acquainted with all sides of their common humanity. There are many blots upon it. It is often very unreasonable and unmanageable. It will not see the right unless it may use its own eyes. It will cling to the wrong until it sees fit to drop it. But when we feel that this wayward human nature has made better laws, and better governments, than were ever made for it; when we remember who set this race in the world, and that His judgment will adequately settle all moral questions with His creatures; and when we consider that we can recognize no weakness in others, except by the mirror within ourselves, we need not blush to accept our common brotherhood, and feel all the more sure of it because of our own imperfections. When the great mass moves on, it is worth something to be able to guide and accelerate its motion.

But nations have other things to consider beyond their own home policies. There is an outer as well as an inner life, which they must live, in obedience to law. They, too, are members of a larger commonwealth, and subject to its censures. The law of nations is of binding force upon all civilized people. The government which infringes this ultimate code, subjects itself to the ultimate argument of war. Our experience is too recent for us to require any reminding of the services those men render to their country, who save it in its peril from threatening complications, and keep a justly excited people from letting reasonable anger at other powers lead to unreasonable extremes. From the beginning of our national life until now, American diplomatists have succeeded in accomplishing at least as much real advantage for our nation, and its interests, as has been reaped by any others. We have succeeded in reaching nations whose doors had before been shut against the world. We have induced them to accept for their guidance the systems which have governed others. We have opened discussion, and obtained action, on subjects which may change the moral aspect of the law of nations itself. And yet all other countries have been served by diplomatists, who have been educated from boyhood in that special service, while our ministers and statesmen have all been thrown, untried, into that perilous business. Why have we been safe in following such an unprecedented method?

It is simply because the practice of the law in the United States involves questions analogous to those of the law of nations, in its daily routine. The comity of nations, the conflict of laws, the incidents of domicil, the extent of territorial jurisdiction over persons and property, and a host of other topics on which the civilians have wasted reams of speculation, are as familiar to an American lawyer as the laws of negotiable paper. Our constitution, in regulating the relations of States, and the conditions of property and intercourse, has left a large share of our rights and obligations to be either governed or interpreted by the analogies of International Law. Every lawyer becomes directly or indirectly acquainted with the principles underlying all this subject, and finds it all the more simple, because it is based on no written code, but rests on broad rules of justice, and on the results of general experience. Reasoning from such premises is no strange task to one who must often expound and elucidate constitutional principles, and who has always found it necessary to know something of public usages and policies. The habits of political thought and discussion complete the preparation; and we have abundant reason to feel assured, that those who study legal diplomacy, as a branch of the general system of the law, where it naturally belongs, are not its worst students.

Instead, therefore, of regarding your profession as designed merely to enable one man to get justice against another, by the aid of a feed agent, you can only appreciate its true dignity, when you regard all human law as a connected system, of any part of which you may become the expounders. Public law and private law act reciprocally. Each exists for the sake of the other. The Law of Nations is made for the benefit of the countries subject to it, just as municipal law is made for the people's benefit. But the law which protects and regulates the people strengthens the body politic also, and the law which keeps nations from excesses advances the prosperity of the world. And that law, therefore, may, in its turn, more easily approximate to the general precepts of the higher system which connects the Universe with the celestial throne.

You have no reason to question the utility of such a ministry. Neither have you any occasion to be deterred from it because the field is so great and the labor so continuous. You need never fear to aim to high. The arrow never gravitates upward. The great danger among lawyers is, that they sometimes aim too low. The law, as you have seen, has only its skeleton in law-books. Its body is built up by feeding on human converse, and all profound and elegant learning, and all true philosophy, and all divine morality. While your time should not be spared from immediately legal studies, you can never grow to greatness unless you also find leisure for other acquirements and accomplishments. Nothing is out of place in a lawyer, which can strengthen or embellish the character of a man.

CPSIA information can be obtained at www.ICGtesting.com
Printed in the USA
LVOW10s2101150114

369567LV00005B/397/P

9 781418 191290